Also by William Jay Smith

POETRY

Poems
Celebration at Dark
Poems 1947-1957
The Tin Can and Other Poems
New and Selected Poems
The Traveler's Tree: New and Selected Poems
Collected Poems: 1939-1989
The World below the Window: Poems 1937-1997

For Children

Laughing Time: Collected Nonsense
Boy Blue's Book of Beasts
Puptents and Pebbles: A Nonsense ABC
Mr. Smith and Other Nonsense
What Did I See?
Typewriter Town
Ho for a Hat!
Around My Room

CRITICISM AND MEMOIRS

The Spectra Hoax
The Streaks of the Tulip: Selected Criticism
Army Brat: A Memoir

TRANSLATIONS

Poems of a Multimillionaire by Valery Larbaud
Selected Writings of Jules Laforgue
Collected Translations: Italian, French, Spanish, Portuguese
The Moral Tales of Jules Laforgue
(with Leif Sjöberg) *Agadir* by Artur Lundkvist
(with Leif Sjöberg) *Wild Bouquet: Nature Poems* by Harry
   Martinson

THE CHEROKEE LOTTERY

A SEQUENCE OF POEMS

by

William Jay Smith

CURBSTONE PRESS

Seven of the poems in this sequence were first printed in *The World below the Window: Poems 1937-1997* by William Jay Smith, the Johns Hopkins University Press, 1998; one other appeared in *New Letters*, vol. 65, no. 3; two others in *The Review* (London), vol. 4, no. 5. Other acknowledgments listed on Page 93.

Printed on acid-free paper by Transcon Printing/Best Book, in Canada

The engraving on the cover by Albert Dupont first appeared in *Le Sentier* (The Trail) by William Jay Smith, translated by Alain Bosquet, published by l'Inéditeur (Paris), copyright © 1999 by Albert Dupont.

This book was published with the support of the Connecticut Commission on the Arts, and donations from many individuals. We are very grateful for this support.

Library of Congress Cataloging-in-Publication Data

Smith, William Jay, 1918-
   The Cherokee lottery : a sequence of poems / by William Jay
   Smith.
      p.   cm.
Includes bibliographical references.
ISBN 1-880684-66-7
   1. Cherokee Indians—History—19th century —Poetry. 2.
Cherokee Indians—Relocation—Poetry. 3. Trail of Tears, 1838—
Poetry. 4. Cherokee Indians—Poetry. I. Title.

   PS3537.M8693 C47 2000
   811'.54—dc21   00-026236

published by
CURBSTONE PRESS   321 Jackson Street   Willimantic, CT 06226
         phone: (860) 423-5110   e-mail: info@curbstone.org
                  http://www.curbstone.org

To the memory of

my mother, Georgia Ella Campster,

who was proud of her Choctaw heritage,

and

to the memory of

Edgardo Beascoechea Aranda,

college classmate and descendant of the conquistadors

CONTENTS

The Cherokee Lottery

Journey to the Interior

He has gone into the forest,
to the wooded mind in wrath;
he will follow out the nettles
and the bindweed path.

He is torn by tangled roots,
he is trapped by mildewed air;
he will feed on alder shoots
and on fungi: in despair

he will pursue each dry creek-bed,
each hot white gully's rough raw stone
till heaven opens overhead
a vast jawbone

and trees around grow toothpick-thin
and a deepening dustcloud swirls about
and every road leads on within
and none leads out.

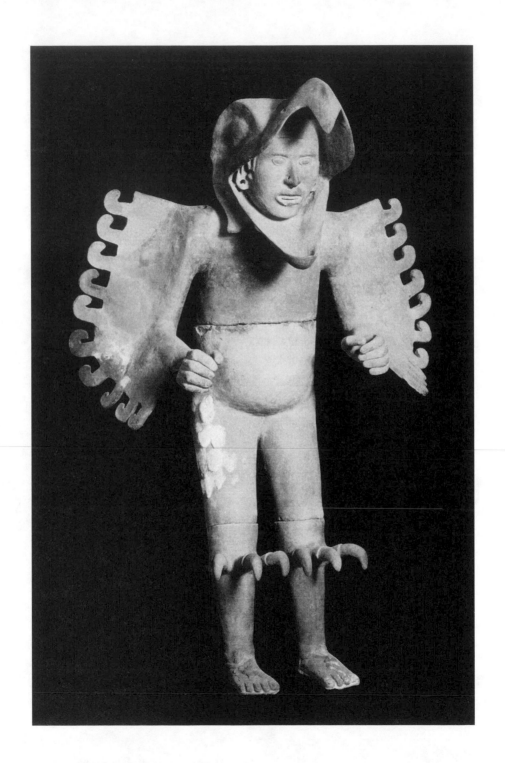

I The Eagle Warrior: An Invocation

This life-size ceramic man costumed as an eagle,
fired clay of a warm tan, with traces
     of applied white plaster,
preserved because the conquistadors,
     on their arrival in the city
of the Aztecs, had thrown it into the lake,
the fierce bird's head covering the man's head
     like a helmet,
the man's head resting within
     the wide protruding beak,
eyes staring from the bird's mouth,
and all along the outstretched arms,
     wings (scalloped, hooked
projections), wind-scoops to catch the air,
three great claws jutting from each knee,
the entire figure leaning forward
     as from some cloud-encrusted crag,
ready to glide, imperial, into the wind . . .

O Eagle-warrior, surrogate of the sun,
     fly off in my mind now
to circle the sun, that "ascending eagle,"
and with your penetrating eye
and your calligraphic wing-span
     printed high upon the air,

follow the westward movement
     of every vanquished tribe.
O Eagle-warrior, quick-eyed, fierce-beaked,
     tense-taloned,
be their emblem, be their witness, be their scribe.

In 1828 gold was discovered on Cherokee land at Dahlonega, in northern Georgia. Where the Cherokees for centuries had hunted, now they grew corn, cotton, squash, and beans, and tended lush peach orchards and rich cattle farms. But still they did not own Dahlonega "just because they had seen it from the mountain or passed it in the chase," so President Andrew Jackson, former Indian fighter, then decreed. In May 1830, at Jackson's prodding, Congress passed the Removal Act, which set aside, in territory west of the Mississippi, districts "for the reception of such tribes or nations of Indians as may choose to exchange the lands where they now reside and remove there." But the Indians had no choice: eight years later, when all resistance had failed, most of the eighteen thousand Cherokees joined the other southern tribes—Choctaws, Chickasaws, Creeks, and Seminoles—in forced exile, where thousands died on what became known as the Trail of Tears.

II   The Cherokee Lottery

"The Cherokee Nation . . . is a distinct community,
occupying its own territory . . . which the citizens of
Georgia have no right to enter, but with the assent of the
Cherokees themselves, or in conformity with treaties
and with the acts of Congress."
>   —Chief Justice John Marshall
>   The United States Supreme Court, 1832

"John Marshall has made his decision: now let him
enforce it."
>   —Andrew Jackson
>   President of the United States, 1832

Georgia 1838

When the Cherokees refused to leave,
the state set up a lottery
to rid them of their land:
a clumsy wooden wheel
sat poised above great black
numbers painted on bright squares—
woodpecker red and watermelon green,
wild azalea orange
and morningglory blue—
to designate the farms
that now were up for grabs:
and while the wheel creaked
slowly round, the Georgians
danced and sang:
"All we want in this creation
is a pretty little girl
and a big plantation
way down yonder
in the Cherokee Nation!"
and laughed until they cried.

General Winfield Scott,
blue-uniformed, bushy-browed, six-foot-three,
arrived from Washington
and addressed the Cherokees:

"May's full moon
           is already on the wane,
and before another
           passes, every Cherokee,
man, woman, and child,
           must move along to join
their brothers in the West."

And when his troops swept in
           from every quarter,
fixed bayonets flashing in the sun
           to roust them from their tables
and their beds,
           the Cherokees, stripped
of everything they owned,
           at last lined up to go.

White-haired Going Snake,
           the eighty-year-old chief,
on his pony led the way,
           followed by young men on horseback.
Then the women and children,
           with the rustling sound
wind makes in tall dry grass,
           came on, and no one spoke,
no one cried: only the dogs
           howled as if they alone

could voice the nation's grief
           while the procession slowly wound its way
off through the tall pines
           over the red clay.

At the moment they began to move,
           a low rumble of distant thunder
broke directly westward
           and a dark spiral cloud rose
above the horizon,
           but the sun was unclouded,
the thunder rolled away,
           and no rain fell.

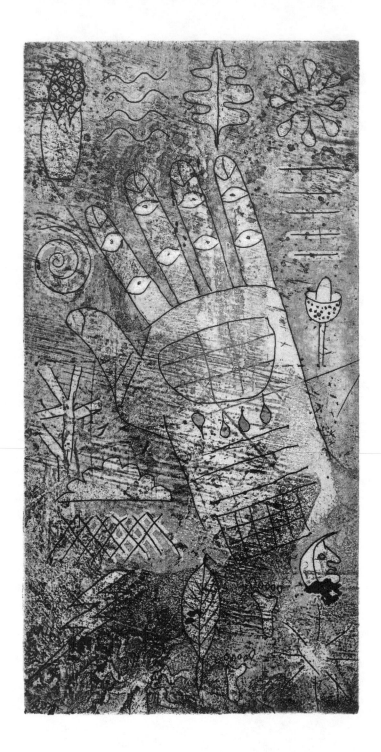

III   The Trail

Past corn
        brown-tasseled
shredded
        against gray sky
yellow hickory
        bronze oak
hairy spiraled
        moss falling
wind-driven
        black boughs
bending over
        black water
twisted vines
        circling
red clay
        burrows
wrinkled
        leaves blowing
dark clouds
        massing
thunder
        splitting
lightning
        forking
torsades
        of rain
falling

                    bright jagged
edges lost
                    in mist rising
above all
                    that human hand
with its
                    central eye
bright
                    forked eye
reaching
                    down
leading
                    deeper on
into
                    dark swamps
tears
                    constant flowing
salt scene
                    never-ending
tear
                    trail

IV   The Talking Leaves: Sequoyah's Alphabet

On February 21, 1827, in New Echota, Georgia, the
capital of the Cherokee Nation, appeared the first issue
of the Cherokee Phoenix, *a newspaper printed part in*
English and part in characters of the alphabet invented
by Sequoyah. The most nearly complete file of the
Cherokee Phoenix *in existence today is one of the*
prized possessions of the British Museum, in London.

"Sequoyah is celebrated as an illiterate Indian genius
who, solely from the resources of his mind, endowed a
whole tribe with learning; the only man in history to
conceive and perfect in its entirety an alphabet or
syllabary."

—Grant Foreman

i

Alone for hours on end, he meditated on his mission:
    to tame the wild beast that for many years
    kept pacing back and forth within his head,

the beast of language, whose every murmur, growl, and hiss
    he knew so well; awake at night, he often felt
    its forked teeth closing down upon him.

He knew that one day he must master it so fully
        it would kneel complaisant at his feet
        and offer up its lurking magic syllables

so he might scratch them down on bark or stone
        and carry them great distances and thus teach
        the Cherokees to talk on paper as white people did.

ii

A silversmith and painter, with one lame leg,
        he'd been a soldier, having fought
        in the Battle of Horseshoe Bend against the Creeks

in 1814, and four years later joined a group
        of some three hundred followers of the Cherokee Chief
        John Jolly on flatboats down the Tennessee,

Ohio, and finally the Mississippi, and drifting
        for long days on those muddy rivers
        toward the good land promised in the west,

he studied the configuration of the clouds
        converging over him, the patterns of the constant
        water curling round the edge, and traced

on them and on the trees the evening campfire fringed
        with light the markings of those sounds
        he would one day record. Reviled and cursed

and taken by his people for a lunatic
        with some diabolic plan that would destroy
        the nation, exiled to a cabin overrun with weeds

and briars, he labored on until he had finally put down
        an alphabet, a system in which single letters—
        eighty-six—would stand for syllables

and from them words could easily be compounded.

iii

To put his crazy notion to a final public test,
        the leaders of the Cherokees had Sequoyah
        and his son, who'd learned his alphabet,

stand far apart, and messengers take sentences
        dictated to each one and then demanded that the other
        read them out as if he'd spoken them himself.

Sequoyah proved his point; and over night as by a miracle
        a thousand Cherokees began to read their language;
        the countryside became a classroom:

without books, blackboards, or charts, they learned
    from one another, making marks on red clay and on stones
    beside the mountain streams and on their cabin walls

till very soon, released as by some unexpected wind,
    the talking leaves flew back and forth from east
    to west and Sequoyah's name was blessed on every tongue

iv

On the high slopes of the Sierra Nevada in central California
    a giant evergreen now bears his name:

SEQUOIA SEMPERVIRENS

Its rings record lost kingdoms, ancient wars,
through raging fires it stood and bears the scars,
yet climbs the mountainside to touch the stars.

"Murder is murder and somebody must answer, somebody must explain the streams of blood that flowed in the Indian country in the summer of 1838. Somebody must explain the four-thousand silent graves that mark the trail of the Cherokees to their exile. I wish I could forget it all, but the picture of six-hundred and forty-five wagons lumbering over the frozen ground with their cargo of suffering humanity still lingers in my memory."

> —John G. Burnett
>   United States Army
>   interpreter on the
>   Trail of Tears, recorded ca. 1890

V   Old Cherokee Woman's Song

They have taken my land,
they have taken my home;
they have driven me here
to the edge of the water.
Cold is the ground
and cold the red water.
At night the men come
to circle the campground;
they carry tall reeds,
each topped with a feather,
a bright eagle feather
to draw our eyes upward
and bring us all hope
for the bitter long journey.
But for me the reed's broken
and the sky it has fallen
where black storm clouds gather.
Cold is the ground
and cold the red water.
My blood it will mix
with the flowing red water:
they have taken my land,
they have taken my home;
I go now to die
beyond the red water.

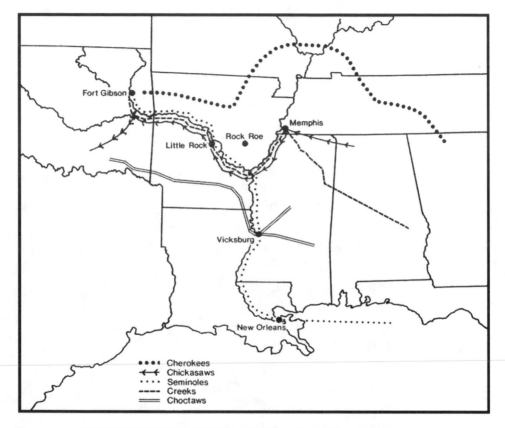

INDIANS OF THE SOUTHEAST: SOME ROUTES OF REMOVAL

VI   The Crossing

"There were among them [a band of Choctaws] the
wounded, the sick, new-born babies, and old men on
the point of death. They had neither tents nor wagons,
but only some provisions and the sight will never fade
from my memory. Neither sob nor complaint rose from
that silent assembly."

—Alexis de Tocqueville
Mississippi, 1831

That winter the southern land had all the contours
of a giant beast in the throes of a convulsion,
its writhing body creased with deep, soft folds
exuding waterfalls like tears and gasping for air;
and into its mouth over the wide rippling tongue
of the great brown river frothing at the edges,
I watched the rafts of the Choctaws
with their hunched and silent burden—
women with babies at their breasts,
old men holding on with withered arms,
small children at their knees—
with never a word of protest,
all borne quietly as if over the world's rim
into the throat of the beast.

VII   The Pumpkin Field

*An Army Lieutenant observes the Cherokees he guards on their
passage to the west, Arkansas 1838*

What a grand lot they were,
        the Cherokees I first saw in June,
lined up in their Georgian camp
        to greet the chief on their departure,
elegant blankets hanging loose
        about their shoulders, ramrod-straight,
dark eyes darting from high-boned
        copper faces under bright turbans
and striped caps pulled down at an angle,
        some in long robes, some in tunics,
all with sashes or wondrous drapery,
        they stood, framed by bearded oaks,
Old Testament patriarchs
        pausing on their way to the Promised Land.

Then in October, where I'd been sent ahead
        to patrol their passage here in Arkansas,
they came from a cold and threadbare wood,
        thin pines bent and tipped with sleet,
eyes glazed and blank,
        half-naked, barefoot,
bones poking through
        their scarecrow shredded clothing,
and stumbled through layers of mist

            onto a scraggly open field
where in wet and tangled grass
            fat pumpkins lay in rows
like painted severed heads.

Oblivious to all around them,
            skeletal automatons,
the Cherokees plunged ahead
            until a farmer on the edge
bade them halt
            and, breaking off a pumpkin,
invited them to take
            whatever his poor field could offer.

Flies swarming to their target,
            they darted up and down the rows,
black hair flying,
            long-nailed tentacles
protruding, they ripped apart
            the pumpkin flesh
until their brown and vacant
            faces merged with jagged pulp,
seeds foaming from
            their hungry mouths, and all I could see,
as on some battlefield, was
            everywhere a wasted mass of orange flesh.

A light rain then began to fall
        as if the shredded pumpkin fiber
drifted down around us:
        I felt ill
and sensed that cholera
        had set in. The farmer guided
me inside his cabin
        and put me down in a dark corner
where between the logs
        I could empty my stomach.

All night long I lay there
        while wind roared
and rain beat down
        and through it I could hear the sloshing
of the weary feet,
        the creak and rattle of ox-carts,
the cursing of the drivers,
        cracking their long whips to urge the oxen on,
the whinnying of horses
        as they struggled through the mud.

"What have we done to these people?"
        I cried out . . . And then a silence fell;
across the dark I saw
        row after row of pumpkins carved and slit,

their crooked eyes
     and pointed teeth all candle-lit within,
not pumpkins but death's-heads they were
     with features of the vacant
hungry faces I had seen,
     stretching to infinity
and glowing in the dark—
     and glowing still when I awoke—

as they do now, and as they always will.

VIII The Buzzard Man

On the Trail an old Choctaw remembers

In the old days, when a Choctaw died,
      his body, wrapped in a bearskin,
lay on a scaffold
      in the open air beside his house,
and there it stayed
      until the flesh had almost
all decayed,
      and then the bone-picker—
hattak fullih nini foni—
      mounted the scaffold to do his work.

The nails of the bone-picker's
      thumb, index, and middle fingers,
never trimmed, flintlike tore
      the remaining flesh
from the cadaver's bones;
      and we waited there below,
and while the picker's eagle
      talons flew, wailing, we echoed
his unearthly moans; until at last
      he bundled up the body's clean remains
and brought them down
      and bore them off to the village
bone house—*a-bo-ha fo-no*—
      where, with the bones of others,
they would stay.

We burned the scaffold
     and marched ahead
into a clearing where,
     at a table spread,
we feasted,
     and solemnly praised the dead.

When the bone house filled,
     the village gathered,
and wailing and crying
     then a long time more,
carried the bones
     to what was sacred ground
and buried them
     in a conical mound.

We changed our ways
     when the white man came:
we placed our dead
     beneath a smooth
pole daubed with red,
     seated upright,
a dark grape vine
     looped around the pole
to ease the spirit
     to its rest.

Now as they march us
　　　　to the west,
we abandon our dead
　　　　along the way—
with no red pole,
　　　　no dark grapevine
to mark their graves—
　　　　and only our tears
to seal our trail.

But on clear nights, outlined
　　　　in the cold against a flaking
sycamore, I follow still the shadow
　　　　of the bone-picker's nail;
and in my heart I feel his claw,
　　　　and on the wind I hear his wail.

IX   Christmas in Washington with the Choctaw Chief

Washington, DC, December 24, 1824

i

Pushmataha, the great Choctaw chief, arrived in Washington
        on December 15, 1824, with his fellow chief Mushalatubbee
        and seven other Choctaw leaders.

He came, he said, "to brighten the chain of peace between
        the Americans and the Choctaws"; and brighten it he did
        at Tennison's elegant hotel, where the holiday

was celebrated in great style with scented wreaths and garlands
        everywhere and a log fire blazing in the hall
        for General Push, as he was called, if he had anything,

had style. When he sat that week to have his portrait painted
        by Charles Bird King, he wore the Brigadier General's
        uniform presented to him by Andrew Jackson,

at whose side he'd fought in 1812 against the English and the Creeks,
        that uniform with golden epaulettes, a belted sword
        and silver spurs, and peaked by a black felt hat

with nodding ostrich feathers. Because of his quick movements
        and his many daring exploits, the Choctaws sometimes
        called him *koi hosh* (the panther) and at other times

oka chilohonfah (falling water) because of his sonorous voice,
    which he'd raised once before in Washington
    when at a government reception Andrew Jackson

asked how it was the chief had gained such stature
    in his tribe. Pushmataha answered first that it was none
    of Jackson's business, but when asked a second

and a third time, he told the interpreter to say, if the white
    chief had to know, that he had neither father
    nor mother, but far away in the great forest

of the Choctaw nation a dark cloud one day rose out of the west
    and when it reached its peak and covered the whole sky
    and wild winds roared and thunder broke and

a sudden savage flash of lightning struck a giant oak
    and cut it straight in two from top to bottom, then from
    that great divided trunk

there stepped a mighty warrior—perfect in stature, profound
    in wisdom, and in bravery unequaled—and this was
    Pushmataha . . . Brave warrior here for peace,

he would accept the Christian call to celebrate:
    so up and down the dim-lit stairs the waiters went
    with flashing trays of food and drink,

oysters on the half-shell, ale and brandy,
        bottles of red wine and whiskey, gin slings,
        and finally, the season's specialty,

huge bowls of egg-nog, day and night, to the sound
        of Christmas caroling, up and down the stairs
        the waiters went until the great Chief

left to visit President Monroe. "Father," he said,
        "I have been here many days, but have not talked,
        I have been sick . . .

None of my ancestors, nor any of my present nation, ever
        fought against the United States. We have given
        of our country to them until it has become quite small.

I came here years ago when I was young to see my Father
        Jefferson. He told me then if ever we got into trouble
        we must come and tell him, and he would help us.

We are in trouble now, and we have come." But the thought
        of any trouble he left far behind him when he later
        went to call on General Lafayette, like him a visitor

that week in Washington: "Even in our remote land, we have
        heard of your great deeds in defense of this country.
        We wanted very much to see you. We have taken

you by the hand and are satisfied. This is the first time
        I have seen you and I feel it will be the last.
        The earth will separate us forever—farewell."

The next day when Pushmataha stepped out of Tennison's Hotel,
        it had begun to snow, and, dizzied by the swirling flakes,
        he fell to the street. His companions carried him

back to his room, and there on Christmas Eve, before he breathed
        his last, he said: "I am dying and will never return
        to my beloved land. When you go there, you will be asked,

'Where is Pushmataha?' and you will answer, 'He is dead,'
        and your words will fall on the ears of my people
        like the sound of a mighty oak falling in the solitude

of the forest . . . When I am dead, let the big guns
        be fired over me."

ii

His wish was granted: on Christmas Day a funeral procession
        a mile long, headed by the United States Marine Band,
        the Senate Chaplain and Colonel McKenney

of the Indian Department, followed by the Choctaw Nation's
        delegates, with Major Pitchlynn, the interpreter,
        Congressmen and citizens of Washington City,

wound its solemn way to the Congressional Cemetery,
  where Captain Dyers' company of riflemen fired
  three volleys over his grave

and Pushmataha was buried with the honors normally accorded
  a United States Major General. Andrew Jackson
  called the Choctaw Chief the "greatest and the bravest

Indian he had ever known," and John Randolph, of Roanoke,
  pronouncing his eulogy in the Senate, said of him
  that he was "wise in counsel, eloquent in an extraordinary

degree, and on all occasions and under all circumstances
  the white man's friend."

iii

The United States government billed the Choctaw delegation
  five thousand dollars for the week it spent at Tennison's
  Hotel, which included $2,149.50 for liquor, $1,134

for clothing, $400 for laundry, $75 for the bootblack, and $58
  for the barbershop. There was no charge for the five
  yards of cloth for the Chief's shroud nor for

the seven-dollar wooden coffin nor for the Congressional
  Cemetery burial plot.

iv

Before leaving Washington, the Choctaw chiefs had ceded
  to the United States all their land east
  of the modern boundary between Arkansas and Oklahoma.

X   At the Theater: The Death of Osceola

Charleston, South Carolina
January 6, 1838

The theater was packed, and just before the curtain rose
    on the comedy *Honeymoon*, a hush went over
    the crowd: a group of Army officers

entered, and at their center, the tall dark Seminole chief
    Osceola, his turban topped with egret plumes, silver
    gorgets hanging from his throat,

their prisoner at Fort Moultrie on Sullivan's Island
    off Charleston Harbor, who had declared:
    "When I make up my mind, I act.

If I speak, what I say I will do. If the hail rattles,
    let the flowers be crushed. The oak will lift up its head
    to the sky and the storm, towering and unscathed."

In October 1837 when several Seminole chiefs had been taken
    prisoner, General Jesup sent word to Osceola
    that he wanted to talk;

and when Osceola came out of the woods, carrying a flag
         of truce, Jesup's deputy General Joseph Hernandez
         ignored it, and took him captive, saying:

"I wish you well, but we have been deceived so often
         that now you must come with me. You will see
         the good treatment that you will experience;

you will be glad that you fell into my hands." Osceola's
         first good treatment was to be thrown into chains
         at the heavy stone Castillo de San Marcos

which the Spaniards had built at St. Augustine. There
         in his dark cell he remembered how not long before
         he had waited until General Wiley Thompson,

who had held his wife in chains, strolled out with his assistant
         after dinner to smoke Cuban cigars under the oaks.
         He had shot Thompson, stabbed him, cut off his head

and carried it back to Wahoo swamp, where amid the cypresses,
         water oaks, and pines, with leathery green vines
         festooning the treetops, he had placed it on a pole.

His men had built a fire below and danced around in victory:
         one of them had climbed up on a stump and imitated
         Wiley Thompson's Georgian drawl: "Those Indians

who do not go peaceably the Great Father will remove by force."

ii

Weakened by malaria, Osceola contracted a sore throat, but
        refused to take the medicine offered by Dr. Weedon
        (he had learned that the doctor's sister

Mary Weedon had been the wife of Wiley Thompson). He chose
        to be treated only by a Seminole medicine man.
        On January 27, 1838, Osceola was so ill

that George Catlin, who had painted his portrait,
        and some officers sat up with him all night. Catlin left
        Charleston two days later, thinking that Osceola

would recover. But the following morning, when it was clear
        that the Chief was dying, he summoned his two wives
        and his two children and dressed himself

in his ceremonial costume: he thrust his arms into the calico
        shirt and eased his legs into their deerskins; he buckled
        on his war belt, his bone powder horn and donned

his turban, the egret plumes of which brought back
         the scent of jasmine and of high epidendrum orchids
         in the tangled trees, the stillness of the Everglades,

where ivory-billed woodpeckers flashed their red, white,
         and blue feathers and the Seminole canoes cut through
         the black water, where little turtles sunned themselves

on moss-rimmed logs, where at night the sickle of the moon
         had ridden over the black night like one of the giant
         silver gorgets he now put on to meet his death.

A warrior he lived, and a warrior he would die: he streaked
         his face and then his neck and ailing throat, his wrists
         and the backs of his hands with red ochre,

then he rose and shook the hands of Dr. Weedon
         and of the attendant officers who lifted him back in bed;
         he pulled the scalping knife from his belt

and laid it across his chest; he took one last long breath
         that had the hollow sound of black swamp water lapping
         the tangled edge of a grass-fringed hammock.

When the others left, Dr. Weedon stayed on. He severed
Osceola's head from his neck, then placed both head
and body in a coffin, tying a scarf around the neck.

Before the funeral, he lifted the head out and shut the coffin
tight. Soon Osceola's head hung in St. Augustine
in Dr. Weedon's house just as Wiley Thompson's head

had bobbed on its pole in Wahoo Swamp. Whenever his young
sons misbehaved, Osceola's head was hung on the bedpost
of their room. When his daughter married, the doctor

presented the head to his son-in-law, who, in turn, gave it
to Dr. Valentine Mott, head of the New York University
Medical School. "I am aware," he wrote,

"that classic lands of Greece and Rome, the isles of the sea,
and many a well-fought field of Europe, have alike given
up their evidences of life,

and in your cabinet of heads we travel into the distant past
and hold communion with those times that were."
When a fire swept through the university museum,

Osceola's head, along with the others in the doctor's cabinet,
went up in flames.

XI The Players

In May 1840, during the Second Seminole War, the players of a traveling Shakespearean troupe left their baggage unattended near St. Augustine, Florida, and a band of Seminoles made off with it into the swamp. The following March at Fort Cummings, the Seminole Chief Coachoochee ("The Wild Cat") and his followers appeared to discuss a treaty with General Walker Keith Armistead, Commander of the United States forces. Coacoochee came forward wearing on his brow the ostrich feathers of Hamlet, Prince of Denmark, and his followers were ornamented with the spangles and bright-colored vests that form the basis of the present-day costume of the Seminoles, who withdrew into the Everglades and never surrendered. Hamlet's headgear became the badge of the Seminole medicine man

A curtain of green divides—and there they are:
the Wildcat Hamlet, black-caped, plumed, and nodding,
Horatio at one side, and on the other,
in silken turban, an opal at one ear, Othello—
or is he the slave who fled the Georgian whip?—
then Richard, grim and brooding in his royal purple,
together with the Fool, whose cap and bells
capture the faintest breeze like wind-chimes . . .
and slowly they advance toward you, General,
seated before your table in the clearing.

Stiff-pleated, soldiers gape;
a bugle sounds; the drummer taps his drum
as if for the cortege of a fallen comrade.

The curtain divides, but, General, for you
dream and reality converge; and reason slumbers.
Your nightmare surfaces; your enemy has risen from the swamp.

And with the drumbeat, rain that you have heard
these many months upon the barracks roof,
a steady tap-tap-tap-tap, then stopping . . . tap . . . tap . . .
tap . . . and then again tap-tap tap-tap,
as unending as the oratory on the Congress floor
to justify an unjustifiable war, to round up
a few Indians, burn their crops and bribe them
to be herded onto ships at Tampa

and carried westward to a barren dust bowl . . .
You hear the constant sloshing of your troops
through ever-present water . . .

. . . and lifted to your steady gaze, the swamp's black mirror,
cut by alligator-blade and skeletal palmetto,
swathe of egret feathers, the heron's bony legs,
dainty stag hoof, dank panther paw, the seething saw grass,
the fangs of water moccasins, the smear of glutinous eggs,
a swarm of black flies circling the even blacker water
like a convocation of Jesuits,
croaking frog-chorale that kept you company at midnight,
the fret and freckle of the water round the grass-fringed
          hammock,
the woodpecker's crimson vest, the spider's velvet net,
all the sequins and the spangles of that savage light,
the rich, wild, ranging necklaces of root,
green, unfolding fans, striped scarves, and spotted feathers,
the stately live oak trailing Spanish moss
(the shredded rags of Lear upon the heath),
the cypress knees protruding from the water
(the knuckles of your fallen dead
whose ghosts have grappled with the mist),
the purple cape of sunset dragging its ermine edge
across the mangrove thicket—
all are mirrored here before you, General: your enemy
has come in the nightmare clothing of the swamp.

Tap . . . tap . . . tap . . .
          Hamlet advances,
holding in one hand a skull—

or is that only a piece of coral from the reef
with all the perforations of the human brain? . . .

You watch it crumble, General, at your feet,
while your Euclidian table projects into the waning light,
and the paper beneath your eagle-talon
rests, a white, fallen feather.

—A wild wind rakes your fort, a hurricane
across the tense peninsula . . .
                    and in the silent eye
a voice that cleaves the quiet water:

"There will be no surrender, General. There will be no peace;
only the murderer who waits, only the poetry that kills."

XII   The Choctaw Stick-Ball Game

Oklahoma, 1834
A traveling painter* remembers

During a period of several sunsets, by the cleansing
    light of the moon, the medicine men of the opposing
    villages undertook the purification

of the players with a sacred scarring of their arms
    and legs, preparing to instill them with the panther's
    speed and the cunning of the small raccoon.

* George Catlin

Then from opposing encampments at dark came a procession
    of torches with notching flames that cut the field
    and caught the stars

and while the women chanted to the dense drum beat,
    the players, shouting heavenward and rattling
    their ball-sticks like a forest

of thunder-struck bamboo, began the ball dance
    that lasted through the night. The field was chosen
    and prepared, four poles planted two hundred yards

apart, two at each end, inclining outward to a width
    of three feet at the top; the parties from each side
    assembled at the poles, and moved, whooping and leaping,

to the center where, in two rows, they laid down their sticks
    three-feet long and fashioned with basketwork at the end
    in the form of a half-opened hand,

beside the lemon-sized ball, stuffed with deer hair
    and laced with buckskin; and while the sticks
    were down, an hour was spent on betting:

men and women, old and young, staked all they could command—
    crops, ponies, trinkets, moccasins, and sometimes
    part of the very territory that they claimed.

At the center of the field four old medicine men
        smoked ceremonial pipes (the puffs of smoke
        were prayers to the Great Spirit

to keep them impartial judges) and then they tossed
        up the ball and the game began . . .

I watched the champion player as he flew across the field—
        Tulli Okchi Ishko ("he who drinks the juice of stone")
        and the stone's juice

clearly flowed down through his powerful brown body,
        from his long black hair and the sweeping
        mane of multicolored horsehair that circled his neck,

past the leather breech-cloth held around his waist
        by a flashing beaded belt of blue and red
        (the Choctaw's favorite colors)

and arching up behind a tail of quills and horsehair,
        through his heavy thighs and legs, down his outstretched
        arms to his hands, each firmly gripping the cupped sticks,

down to his tense bare feet. I saw him leap, a bird,
        far up beyond another bird, the ball, and met by
        other birds rising from the dusty ground.

I watched them as the sticks and feathers flew,
      and it was as if all the wilderness, the swaying
      boughs, the swirling streams,

the hoots and howls, the braided, falling water—
      all had been collected and contained
      and then released at once upon that field.

I began to sketch the scene but so rapid was the play
                that my pen in rushing out to follow it cut
                this way and that till blood raced

along my page and formed a cobweb that fell apart
                and then I started over and cut through
                the mirror beams the medicine men

cast on the players' bodies to catch the power
                of the sun—and the sun itself
                above the tangled sticks

and arms and legs and feathers became
                itself a ball of fire that dropped
                beyond the poles into the night

and brought an end to that great game
                upon my crumpled, threaded page—
                that ball game that the tribe had called

                "little brother to war."

XIII Song of the Dispossessed

You came across the water,
    like gods you walked ashore;
the fabric of our dreaming
    was the clothing that you wore.

You came with ornament
    far brighter than the sun;
you brought the handsome horse,
    the flashing blade, the gun.

You brought your holy book
    that held a world entire,
a life that never ended;
    and water that was fire.

You said, "We'll live as brothers,
    as brothers we will die;
we'll share the forest carpet
    and the blanket of the sky."

But then when we came near you,
    you said, "Now move away;
you come too close now, brother,
    it's dangerous to stay

so close to one another;
    and you must understand
that we know what is better—
    we'll send you to a land

far richer in the west
        beyond the great brown river
where grass is always green
        and there you'll live forever."

And so you took our country,
        you took our sacred ground,
the birds and beasts we cherished,
        the falling water's sound,

the stag that with his antlers
        breaks the sun-flecked trail,
the mockingbird, the turkey,
        the heron and the quail.

You sent us to this desert,
        this sand, these pitted stones,
where wind rakes through the gully
        and bares the bison's bones,

where now above this barren earth
        your great bald eagle screams,
that robbed us of our country
        and carried off our dreams.

XIV   The Buffalo Hunter

I go to kill the buffalo.
The Great Spirit sent the buffalo
On hills, in plains, and woods.
So give me my bow, give me my bow:
I go to kill the buffalo.
                    —Sioux Hunting Song

Buffalo Bill, Buffalo Bill, never
            misses and never will;
Always aims and shoots to kill,
And the company pays the buffalo bill.
                    —Kansas Pacific Railroad Song

"Here was a world almost without a feature,
            an empty sky, and empty earth,
            front and back . . .

Even my body or my own head seemed a great thing
            in that emptiness—this spacious vacancy,
            the greatness of the air,

this discovery of the whole arch of heaven, this straight
            unbroken prison-line of the horizon—
            the universe laid bare . . ."*

*Robert Louis Stevenson

Nothing moved in this great emptiness
      except gigantic herds of buffalo,
      dark clouds of humped matchstick-legged beasts

sent by the Great Spirit for the survival
      of those Indian tribes that inhabited this desert,
      and those other tribes forced to join them.

Having driven the tribes from the East,
      the white man followed to kill off the buffalo,
      all that remained to keep them alive.

By mid-century hunting buffalo became a mania:
      a Kansas paper wrote: "They come from London—
      cockneys, fops, and nobles—

and from all parts of the Republic to enjoy
      what they call sport. Sport! Where no danger
      is incurred and no skill required."

Among those who came in 1854 was Sir St. George Gore,
      Irish baronet, who had hunted in Africa
      and Asia, and had decided now to try the West.

He came equipped; with him he had:
      21 two-horse charettes (in the West they were called
          Red River carts)
      112 thoroughbred horses
      3 milch cows
      18 oxen
                        and

4 six-mule wagons
2 three-yoke wagons
a green and white striped tent
ten by eighteen feet
complete with carpet
a carved marble washstand
an iron dining table
solid silver drinking cups
embossed with the family crest (a tiger rampant)
one wagonload of firearms
a complete set of Shakespeare

    and

between forty and fifty dogs
mostly greyhounds and staghounds
of the most beautiful breeds

    and

to accompany him came from Ireland
his personal valet whose job it was
to tie the flies when Sir St. George
went fishing

    and

Sir William Thomas Spencer Wentworth-Fitzwilliam,
the sixth Earl of Fitzwilliam,
his great friend, an amateur astronomer,
who came with telescope to scan the western skies.

To guide him on his journey Sir St. George hired
      Jim Bridger ("Ole Gabe"),
      an illiterate but experienced hunter,
      to whom at night he read Shakespeare.

For the next two years Sir St. George scoured Colorado,
      Montana, and Wyoming, during which time he slaughtered
      2,000 buffalo, 1,600 deer and elk, 100 bear
      (including 40 grizzlies).

After finishing off a herd of buffalo, Sir St. George
      would stride among the shaggy corpses, picking out
      those he thought would look best in his trophy room

and he kept several taxidermists as busy as his gun bearers.
      So that he could fish on Pike's Peak he hired
      an entire tribe of Blackfoot Indians to cut a road for him.

When one of his men in Wyoming picked up a gold nugget,
      Sir St. George told him it was *micu*; he had come
      on a *pleasure*, not a *treasure*, hunt.

His 6,000 mile trek had cost him the income for three years
      from his Irish estates; at the end of it he built
      flat boats on the Missouri to carry back his trophies.

When he wanted to sell his equipment and was offered
        only a tenth of what it was worth, he hauled it
        to the top of a bluff, set it on fire,

and handed out rifles to the Indians who came to see him off.

                                    *

When Sir St. George and his entourage passed through
        Leavenworth, Kansas, on his way west, he was admired
        by an eight-year-old boy,

William Frederick Cody, who a little more
        than a decade later signed a contract for $500
        a month to provide buffalo meat for work gangs

on the Kansas-Pacific Railroad, and, as Buffalo Bill,
        shot 4,280 of the woolly beasts. In 1872, as a guide,
        he led General George Armstrong Custer and Philip Sheridan

and the Grand Duke Alexis, son of the czar of Russia,
        on a "Grand Buffalo Hunt." Whenever the Grand Duke
        made a kill, it was celebrated with champagne.

In 1882 he organized an "Old Glory Blowout," a Fourth
        of July celebration in North Platte, Nebraska,
        the forerunner of his "Wild West Show,"

which had its first presentation the next year
        in Omaha. At first a kind of rodeo
        in which gunmanship, roping

and riding predominated, it later included
        enactments of episodes from Western history,
        such as the Pony Express, attacks on stage coaches

and settlers' cabins, and finally "Custer's Last Stand,"
        the defeat at Little Big Horn, in which half the Indian
        cast had participated in the original battle.

                            *

For his 1885-86 season, Buffalo Bill persuaded Sitting Bull
        to join him for his European tour.

XV   Sitting Bull

in Serbia

A hundred years ago, they say, Buffalo Bill
brought his Wild West Show—
and, with it, Sitting Bull—
here to this Serbian town.*

*Vršac

People came to stare at the western warrior,
his weathered face mottled and brown
as a raisin from their vineyards;
and what did he see, the old chief,
when, dark-eyed, he returned their stare?
When the carnival dust settled
and the war whoops died, what did he see
beyond the hoopla of the ring,
the wild, phony, stampeding horses?
In a twisting thread of smoke
rising from the square
he saw perhaps the shrouded mountains of his boyhood;
in the embroidered dresses of peasant women,
the flashing pebbles of clear streams;
in the somber, tasseled jackets of the men
the outline of a circling eagle's wings.
And far off, above the House of the Two Pistols,
where Black George, leader of the Serbian revolt,
had hidden,
high above the Bishop's Palace,
over the town's brooding tower,
he saw the Earth's Great Spirit
hover for a moment,
and then, with a shaggy, humpbacked bison,
plunge down the western sky
headlong into the night.

XVI   The Burning of Malmaison

Greenwood, Mississippi
March 31, 1942

i

On a brisk cool evening when the wind
      had rinsed the sky and the pines
      smelled fresh from rain the night before

the mistress of the house and her sister
      welcomed two guests from town to the gilded
      parlor of Malmaison,

the mansion built a hundred years earlier
      by Greenwood LeFlore, the son
      of a French Canadian trader at the garrison

of Mobile and his part-Choctaw wife. At the age
      of twenty-four he had become the Choctaw Chief
      and ten years later signed

the Treaty of Dancing Rabbit Creek, which ceded
      to the United States most of northern Mississippi
      and sent its Choctaw residents off to Oklahoma.

Greenwood—which in Choctaw *Itta-oke-chunka*
        means "tough hickory"—had stayed behind to build
        at Teoc ("the place of the tall pines")

a mansion named for Empress Josephine's, Napoleon's
        gift to her, and had filled it with
        rich furnishings from France.

The ladies sat on gilt-edged sofas of brocaded
        silk damask across from the marble mantelpiece
        with its gilded candelabra

and its clock of gold and ebony, below which blazed
        a log fire that took the chill off
        the evening, and whose flames

opened and closed on the mirrored walls
        like the fins of tropical fish
        criss-crossing the room's

great clear green pool and bringing an elegant
        freshness from beyond, a freshness
        broken by a sudden rumble

as of thunder on a distant mountain, followed
        by the heavy steady pounding
        of horses' hooves

that grew more deafening until the Corinthian
        columns seemed ready to crack open;
        and the ladies, terrified, could see

themselves held prisoner, the attackers
        bearing in from all sides—they were
        there already pounding from above—

and then a voice called out to them
        from the hallway, a faint crackling,
        a clearing of the throat,

someone trying to call out but cut off
        in the attempt . . . And then they rose
        and pulled the curtains back

to find the moon so bright upon the lawn
        they swore the headlights of a pack
        of circling cars had blinded them,

and turning back to reach the rifle
        hanging in the hall, they stepped
        into the very throat

from which the crackling came, great tongues
        of flame leapt forth while smoke
        poured down and timbers crashed

and they had met their all-consuming enemy head-on.

On the lawn the ladies stood beside the pieces
       they had saved, the boule table,
       the long gilt mirror,

a love seat and six chairs, goblets, tureens, epergnes,
       and candelabra—a sorry bit, an evil
       offering of Malmaison's

French finery, and on top, Greenwood's
       sword and the silver-embroidered belt
       that Andrew Jackson had presented

to him when he was named Choctaw chief,
       and fastened to the scabbard the silver
       medal, a gift of Thomas Jefferson;

on one side the pipe of peace lay across
       a tomahawk and on the other were
       the words "Peace and Prosperity."

The flames swept up into the night,
       lifting the stars as they swirled ever higher,
       the embers from a flaking log,

and the cupola, gigantic red-veined,
       fire-rimmed eyeball fixed on heaven
       crumpled up and sank

and through the hiss, the crackle, and the roar,
        the cracking and the melting of the glass,
        the merging of hot porcelain

and timber, still the ladies heard the pounding
        of the horses' hooves, and the insistent
        thud of marching feet,

the exiled Chocktaw voices that would never cease,
        a century of voices choking
        in the flame and smoke of Malmaison . . .

Since there was nothing more that they could
        rescue from the house, they sent black
        servants to the stable

to save the carriage that had taken Greenwood LeFlore
        to Washington and back, and there it was—
        the solid sterling

trimmings and its ivory tacked silk damask
        upholstery gleaming in the light
        beside the boule table,

the mirrors, and the glass, and the ladies
        turned to it now, a refuge from the inferno
        swirling ever more intense around them,

and sobbing softly, then they took their places,
        waiting, it appeared, for the carriage wheels
        to lift them far above the flames

and off into the crystal night.

iii

In March twenty years later, in the brambles that had
      overgrown the family cemetery, two Boy Scouts
      came upon the headstone that read:

Greenwood LeFlore

Born June 3, 1800
Died August 31, 1865

The last chief of the Choc-
taw Nation east of the
Mississippi River

and seeing that the earth around it had been recently
      disturbed, alerted the family, who days
      later had diggers

go down to a depth of eight feet where they found
      only three pieces of yellow pine,
      broken but intact,

that had perhaps enclosed the grave,
      but the coffin, and, with it, the remains,
      the skull and bones

of the Choctaw chief, had disappeared.
  Beside the headstone in the orange clay
  the diggers unearthed a thin blue vein,

a remnant surely of the stars and stripes
  so dear to the Choctaw chief,
  who, when he was dying,

had asked his granddaughters to come
  and hold the flag above him,
  which they did, and they granted

him his dying wish, to have it wrapped
  around him in his grave, and of it now
  all that was left: this small blue stain.

XVII The Artist* and His Pencil:
A Search for the Purebloods

Northern Oklahoma

*Charles Banks Wilson

Sixty-three Indian tribes were represented in Oklahoma—all
         of them except the indigenous Quapaw
         had originated elsewhere

and they all would gather here to dance. The powwow
         was a means of reliving the old ways, and
         recently returned from Art School in Chicago,

I began to draw the Indians as they danced: the chiefs
         in their buffalo-horn headdresses and their festoons
         of vibrant feathers,

their long black braids and red-painted faces, black
         buffalo tassels, rainbow-colored beadwork,
         shuffling on one foot

and then on another, scuffing up the dust, their eyes
         turned inward as if fixed on a distant mountain
         range that only they could see

and, with every step, could feel it crumble there within,
         body swaying, arms flung out, feet skimming the ground;
         and then the women in fringed buckskin dresses

dancing the traditional buckskin dance, and clad
         in dresses sewn with bright tilted
         metal cones in the jingle-dress dance.

And the men weaving, sinuous and smooth, streamers
      of yarn, in the grass dance; and finally in
      one fancy dance, men padded with double bustles,

ribbons and streamers whirling, colors interweaving
      incessantly, as if they each had gone up in flame,
      the hot coals flying from their feet.

At night two naked bulbs hung over the dancing ground
      to light the dancers, and in the distance
      kerosene lanterns lit up corners of the camp

and the shadows gave the dancers the hooped shapes
      of buffalo and the sharp beaks of circling eagles;
      off to one side was a bright-painted

merry-go-round the Quapaw had provided so their black-eyed
      whooping children could ride the painted horses
      instead of real horses circling a wagon train.

As I watched the children passing on their painted ponies,
      I thought how far off now the real buffalo
      and the eagles that flew above them were.

The dancers were calling back a life that was now long gone,
      and when the dancing stopped, they took off
      their feathered headdresses and donned the blue jeans,

dungarees, cast-off combat khaki, and broad-brimmed hats
        like the rest of us; and as I watched the Indians
        watching Indians, I saw a whole race disappearing

before my eyes: among the dancers were many full-bloods,
        those with the blood of several tribes, but every
        year there were fewer and fewer purebloods,

those full-blooded Indians of only one tribal lineage,
        so I decided then and there to seek them out
        and with my pencil leave the last clear record

of each vanquished tribe. From then on I tracked them down
        to their trailers, their back porches, their hospital
        beds, their churches, and their bars:

the Seneca in the boarding house, one eye half-closed,
        the corners of his mouth drawn severely down,
        holding the turtle-shell rattle that had been brought

by the original Senecas to Oklahoma territory in 1830;
        the Sac and Fox hereditary chief and last original
        allottee, now nearly blind and deaf; his granddaughters

wanted to know how much I would charge *them* to draw his portrait;
        the last Caddo pureblood, whose beautiful daughters
        came in from gathering mushrooms;

perhaps the very last pure Delaware, so intent on posing
        that he fainted dead away—and I thought, "Oh, God,
        I have murdered that last Delaware—"

but then he revived; the Seminole medicine man I found
        at the Veterans' Hospital, 103 years old, too old
        to serve in World War I but he had cut seventeen years

from his age and had gone off anyway; the young Comanche,
        just returned from Vietnam, who was mowing the grass
        at Fort Sill when I found him;

an indomitable Miami woman, bolt upright in her nursing home
        wheelchair; the Menominee on a hot August day
        perched on the edge of his bed

with his menthol rub beside him; Louis Featherman, a Sioux
        from South Dakota, who was dying but had traveled far
        to reach me, to have his portrait done—

"So they will know that I have lived"; the Natchez hereditary
        chief, not a pureblood but more Natchez than any other,
        a living monument to the great Mississippi tribe

that had greeted De Soto; Henry Turkeyfoot, the Shawnee,
        tall and slim, black hair brushed forward almost
        to the bridge of his nose, a tightly rolled

bandanna around his neck, who confessed in a thin high-pitched
        voice that he had seen me before, but not knowing
        my business, had hidden in the bushes

as he did whenever strangers came, whose funeral was held
        beneath a cottonwood tree on which they hung
        hair from his horse's tail and a squirrel skin

to assure him of a good horse to ride, and game to hunt
        in the hereafter; the Osage, whose head rose
        straight up from his neck, having once rested

on a cradle board; the Ponca, a descendant of chieftains,
        who died fighting a grass fire that threatened
        his house; the proud Otoe pureblood,

who, forty-five years earlier, as a six-foot-three,
        two-hundred-fifty-pound man, long hair the color
        of a moonless night and smooth skin as red

as western Oklahoma earth, had been chosen at the Texas Fair
        "the most typical Indian of the Southwest," but who now
        had put away his eagle war bonnet and his beaded

breastplate, his white hair so thinned his braids had to be
        filled with yarn wrappings, his few remaining teeth,
        the yellow kernels of an old corn-cob, and his body

        bent like a battered reed.

In Tulsa I tracked down one of the last pureblood Kaw,
  and found him seated in his driveway listening
  on earphones to peyote music,

and now, with no one left to understand his native tongue,
  he told me, "God gave the Kaw this language, so when
  I talk to people, I speak English,

  but when I talk to God, I speak His language . . .

I am old myself now, older than many of the purebloods
        I sketched a quarter of a century ago,
        and when at night I lie awake recalling

my Quapaw wife, whose tribe once owned all of Oklahoma
        and Arkansas, and I follow in memory
        the fine outline of her face

imprinted in sleep as on a medallion in the moonlight,
        all those other faces that my pencil found so
        long ago return to me,

each one, each untouched tribe, recorded in a never-ending moment,
        distinct and clear.

XVIII   Full Circle: The Connecticut Casino

Foxwoods Resort Casino
Mashantucket Pequot Tribal Nation
Connecticut

21 January 2000

"The Pequots were, historically, one of the most
potent political and military forces on the East
Coast. Now they've come full circle. No one can
say the glory of native culture is a past phenomenon."

— W. Richard West
Director, Museum of the American Indian
Smithsonian Institution

O

  O

    O the first full moon of the year 2000
has risen over the snowbound fields of southeastern Connecticut—
and here—not far from where the much-esteemed memorable
Mayflower deposited her Pilgrims—*In God they trusted*—
on Plymouth Rock,
                    here not far from Mystic,
where in 1627 those same Pilgrims attacked
a fortified village and almost finished off the Pequots,
those Indians they denounced as devil-worshipping witches
destined for damnation,
                        here, caught in the snowdrifts
before the Foxwoods Resort Casino,
erected not long ago by the few remaining descendants
of that once powerful nation,
I find in the bright moonlight a long line
of what appear to be huge brown hairy Quonset huts

or shaggy bloated chocolate eclairs
with two toothpicks at one end and a tassel at the other,
all nudging one another in a vain attempt to move forward
and shake loose from the snow but sinking ever deeper,
and now they come clearly into focus:
a herd of *buffalo*, just as George Catlin had pictured them—
huge creatures, little Titanics each trapped in its own iceberg,
doomed to icy death,
while on their buffalo-hide snowshoes,
buoyant as if on water-skis,
the Indians skim in from every side,
long lances ready for the kill.
I listen to the groans of the dying beasts
and to the litany of the victorious hunters:

> Hi - Ya - Ho
> Here we go
> flying with feathers
> through the snow
> to kill
> the snowbound
> buffalo

until hypnotized by their rhythmic chant
and transfixed by the gushing blood
printing its delicate pink patterns on the snow,

I watch a dark buffalo-colored cloud
move in over the moon,
and when it passes
                    and the snow suddenly melts away,
I realize that what I see is not a herd of *buffalo*
at all, but steaming *buses* queuing up to deliver
their anxious occupants
to the gambling tables of the great Foxwoods Resort Casino;
and once inside
                    the ladies come and go
                    speaking not of Michelangelo
in Rainmaker Square as they file past the two-and-a-half ton
cast-crystal Indian brave, clad only in a breech-cloth,
kneeling on a high rock beside a clear pool
surrounded by lush vegetation,
head tilted up to the glass dome,
his taut bow ready every hour on the hour
when the entire crystal body
is suddenly suffused with the rosy tint of a perfume bottle
to release a laser arrow
that pierces the sky
                    and invariably brings down rain.
They enter a garden of breath-taking color,
inebriating enticement, golden promise, and cascading silver
in the largest casino of the Western Hemisphere
with its five thousand five hundred slot machines,
its Race Book and Sports Bar
where they may place their bets and watch races anywhere
on the most advanced large-screen projectors in the world,
or enter a poker tournament in the finest Poker Room
east of the Mississippi.

It was with this Casino that the Mashantucket Pequot Nation
finally tricked the Great White Father Trickster
or outfoxed the Great White Fox.
It is no accident that the tribe's logo
displays a *small* white fox poised against a tree
perched on a rocky knoll representing Mashantucket,
this "much wooded land" where the natives once hunted and prospered.
The full story of the Fox People's cunning and resilience
is told in a brochure that the gamblers may read between bets
or follow in the dioramas of the new Mashantucket Pequot Museum
that spreads its concrete gray gull wings into the cedar swamp,
where this once powerful people had been left for dead
when the Great White Fox prepared to move in
and take over twenty-five years ago what remained of the reservation.
Then the two old Pequot women, half-sisters, left alone there,
summoned the existing tribe members back to their ancestral home,
where they barely survived in trailers, cutting wood,
growing lettuce, and boiling sap
until, when the tribe won official recognition,
they opened a Bingo Hall, and their worries were over.
Here on this magical night everything has come full circle:
while the gaudy wheels in the slot machines
continue their deafening rounds,
and the white spots on the red and black dice
gallop over the green and purple baize
and the players place their bets in the betting circles
for Black Jack or Let-it-Ride Poker
and the round red and green Foxwoods chips pile high
on the various tables,

high above that table where the spinning ball comes to rest
on the red and black numbers of the roulette wheel,
I hear the faint ghostly creaking of the clumsy wooden wheel
designed more than a century and a half ago
for the Cherokee Lottery in Georgia.
And outside, over the cedar swamp and through the snowbound fields,
I follow in the icy air the misty figures of all those tribes
driven from the East,
led on his pony by white-haired Going Snake,
the eighty-year-old Cherokee Chief,
the Choctaws, Creeks, and Chickasaws,
old men, women with babies knee-deep in the snow,
their ox-carts lumbering over the frozen ground
and farther north, the Kickapoos, the Shawnees, the Delawares,
the Wyandots, the Senecas, the Miamis,
all driven into exile in the winter wind.
A night of bitter memory but also one of celebration
for with the Trickster tricked
and all the gold stolen from the Cherokees in Georgia
seeming to return now to the Pequots in Connecticut,
the moonlight releases those legendary Indian mischief makers,
Rabbit and Coyote, who hop, prance, slink and weave
through the house with their endless bags of tricks:
to create greater and greater excitement
they explode canisters of laughter in every corner
and in their various guises, in dungarees and dinner jackets,
in cowboy hats and Reeboks,
they hover over the gambling tables,
egging the players on to ever-increasing extravagance
in their betting, helping the Fox People,
with the lure of moonlit gold,
to continue to outfox the Great White Fox.

At midnight when the cast-crystal Indian brave's laser arrow
flies up to the glass dome,
the tricksters have arranged a devilish devastating final trick.
The lights go out everywhere in the casino,
a ghostly mist settles down

                     and with it an eerie silence
envelops everything and everybody.
All is in a state of suspension:

the slot machine handles locked in place,
the roulette wheels spun to a dead stop,
the racing screen totally blank
when down from the glass dome
drops the giant bright-colored mask of Coyote,
or, rather, of Ms. Coyote,
(the trickster, consummate cross-dresser, has decided
that this extraordinary occasion requires a feminine presence).
And so, there, lit from every angle by laser blades
of raw white light,
hangs the slender appetizing likeness
of Ms. Coyote's huge face with its piercing red-pupiled brown eyes
set in their empty white sockets,
her mauve-rimmed eyelids and mauve-tinted cheekbones
highlighting the mauve of the brass-studded lining of her ears,
one supporting a freshly-picked white rose,
the other dangling slightly, tipped by its earring,
a bright-beaded tassel
that looks for all the world like an Indian price tag.
From the thin lascivious full-reddened lips drawn back
under the black round rubbery tip of her nose
in a wry sinister smile over the pointed teeth
emerges a voice neither male nor female
but one having a somewhat unsettling sexless and timeless quality
and the cold compact clarity of a computer chip.
Now projected to every corner of the casino
in distinct but drumlike decibels,
                    it makes the following announcement:

All those who are willing and eager to relinquish territory
obtained illegally from Indian tribes at any time in the past
    will kindly
record their property identification numbers on their Wampum
Cards and leave them at the Cherokee Lottery Roulette table.
When their numbers are called, they are requested to proceed
to the Holding Area in front of the Casino. There the
Native American Escort Service will help facilitate their
departure on fully-monitored Buffalo Buses by providing
each one with a TRAIL OF TEARS Passport printed in Cherokee
that will insure their safe passage on the Tall Ships
that await them at the principal ports of the Eastern Seaboard.

And while the announcement is repeated
and the lights go up throughout the Casino
and the rush toward the Roulette Table begins,
I can see the highways black with those buses,
bumper-to-bumper like the buffalo neck-to-neck in the snow,
and I can picture those eager exultant exiles embarking
on the tall ships, which at dawn the next day
with the sky as wind-swept and clear
as it was over the Great Plains
when George Catlin painted it and offered it to the world,
will lift anchor and set off, their sails billowing
in pure joy, for that far-off land
                              where people speak
only the truth
                    and where all races live together
in lasting peace and perfect harmony.

Acknowledgments and Notes

The removal of the Southern Indian Tribes—the great American tragedy of the "Trail of Tears"—has been something of an obsession with me since I first discovered seventy years ago that members of my mother's family in Mississippi, Oklahoma, and Arkansas, by reason of their Choctaw blood, claimed to have played a part in it. I have given the details of that discovery in *Army Brat*, New York: Persea Books, 1980, pp. 109-145, my memoir about the twenty years (1921-1941) spent growing up in and around Jefferson Barracks, Missouri, just south of St. Louis, the United States Army's first permanent base west of the Mississippi. As the son of an enlisted man, a corporal in the Sixth Infantry Band, I concluded then: "While I was brought up on an Army garrison founded as an outpost in the Indian Wars, I knew that I had forebears on the outside and in the enemy's camp, and that knowledge gave me a new strength to face the limited—and limiting—aspects of military life."

My mother, Georgia Ella Campster, encouraged me in my research into her family history, as have my cousins Verlia Fullbright of Arkansas and Gladys Daniels of Oklahoma.

In putting together the poems for *The Cherokee Lottery*, I am grateful for the early encouragement of Eudora Welty, Jacques Barzun, and the late Ralph Ellison. The late James Merrill, after reading some sections of the sequence, arranged for me to receive an Ingram Merrill Foundation grant, which made it possible to travel several times to Arkansas, Oklahoma, and Mississippi, where at Philadelphia I received the assistance of Chief Phillip Martin of the Mississippi Band of Choctaw Indians and of Robert B. Ferguson.

Harold Bloom and Daniel Hoffman offered words of encouragement. Robert Phillips, Daniel Corrie, and Daniel Mark Epstein read early drafts of sections of the sequence and made valuable suggestions.

It was thanks to my college classmate Elizabeth Willems that I discovered *Search for the Purebloods*, with drawings and narrative by Charles Banks Wilson, published by the Oklahoma University Press in 1983 and 1989, which is now being reprinted.

Charles Banks Wilson was introduced to President Harry Truman by Thomas Hart Benton as America's greatest artist historian. Not since George Catlin has any artist drawn, from life, representatives of so many

American Indian tribes. Wilson's work has been exhibited throughout the world. Permanent collections of major museums and galleries contain his paintings, prints, bronzes and ceramics, including New York's Metropolitan and the Philadelphia Art Museum, in Washington, the Library of Congress, the Corcoran, the Smithsonian, the White House, and the National Capitol.

Mr Wilson has graciously allowed me to quote extensively from his book and to add to his own words others that I thought he might have spoken and to reproduce several of his splendid drawings.

I am indebted to my friend, the French painter, Albert Dupont, who did the engraving on the cover especially for this book; it appeared first in *Le Sentier* (*The Trail*) by William Jay Smith, translated by Alain Bosquet, published by l'Inéditeur, Paris, 1999. For the reproduction of her mask "Ms. Coyote" I am indebted also to Jean Lamarr, Paiute/Pit River Indian, and to American Indian Contemporary Arts in whose catalog of the exhibit *Indian Humor*, San Francisco, 1995, it was first reproduced.

Elizabeth Spencer was immensely helpful with the sequence on Chief Greenwood LeFlore, whose descendants she knew personally and to whom she has devoted a chapter in her memoir *Landscapes of the Heart*, New York: Random House, 1998.

My wife Sonja Haussmann, by translating several sections into French, helped clarify the whole sequence; she has followed every detail with care and has maintained from the beginning an inspiring interest in the project.

Books that provided background material

(Of these I am particularly indebted to Gloria Jahoda, *The Trail of Tears*, the first book that I read on the subject, and to Cushman, *History of the Choctaw, Chickasaw and Natchez Indians*, Grant Foreman, *Indian Removal*, and James Wilson, *The Earth Shall Weep: A History of Native America.*)

Jesse Burt and Robert B. Ferguson, *Indians of the Southeast: Then and Now,* Nashville, Tennessee: Abingdon Press, 1982; George Catlin, *North American Indians*, edited and with an introduction by Peter Matthiessen, New York: Viking Penguin, 1989; H.B. Cushman, *History of the Choctaw, Chickasaw and Natchez Indians*, New York: Russell & Russell (Anthenum Publishers), 1962; Arthur H. DeRosier, Jr., *The Removal of the Choctaw Indians*, Knoxville, Tennessee: University of Tennessee Press, 1970; Marjorie Stoneman Douglas, *The Everglades: River of Grass,* St. Simons Island, Georgia: Mockingbird Books, 1974; Grant Foreman, *Indian Removal: The Emigration of the Five Civilized Tribes of Indians*, Norman,

Oklahoma: University of Oklahoma Press, 1932, 1953; Grant Foreman, *Sequoyah*, Norman, Oklahoma: University of Oklahoma Press, 1938; James D. Horan, *The McKenney-Hall Gallery of American Indians*, New York: Crown Publishers, 1972; Gloria Jahoda, *The Trail of Tears*, New York: Holt, Rinehart and Winston, 1975; Edwin C. McReynolds, *The Seminoles*, Norman, Oklahoma: University of Oklahoma Press, 1957; Florence Rebecca Ray and Frances Ray Wagner, *Chieftain Greenwood LeFlore and the Chocktaw Indians of the Mississippi Valley*, Memphis, Tennessee: Davis Printing Company, 1976; Charles Banks Wilson, *Search for the Purebloods*, Norman, Oklahoma: University of Oklahoma Press, 1989: James Wilson, *The Earth Shall Weep: A History of Native America*, New York: Atlantic Monthly Press, 1998: Ronald Wright, *Stolen Continents*, New York: Houghton Mifflin, 1992.

By concentrating on a few of the most dramatic scenes of the Indian removal, I have had to omit reference to the divisions among the Cherokees prior to the final departure in 1838 and to the tragic consequences of that division in Oklahoma. Specific sources for the sequence are listed below:

p. 3 H.B. Nicholson with Eloise Quiñones Keber, *Art of Aztec Mexico: Treasures of Tenochtitlan*, Washington, National Gallery of Art, 1983, p. 85.

pp. 7-9 Jahoda, p. 219, 224, 233-234; Foreman, *Indian Removal*, p. 266; J. Wilson, p. 165.

pp. 13-17 All based on Foreman, *Sequoyah*. The concluding poem "Its rings record. . ." is reprinted from *New Letters*, vol. 65, no. 3.

p. 18 John Burnett, quoted in Grace Steele Woodward, *The Cherokees*, Norman, Oklahoma: University of Oklahoma Press, 1963, p. 125.

p. 19 J. Wilson, pp. 166-167;

p. 21 J. Wilson, p. 166; the first four lines are taken partly from a sentence in Holland Cotter, "A World of Passions, Stroke by Quivering Stroke," *New York Times*, September 3, 1999.

pp. 22-25 I have combined several scenes here to have this occur to the Cherokees in Arkansas. The description of the Cherokees is from journalist John Howard Payne, quoted in Jahoda, p. 221. The speaker is Lieutenant Jefferson Van Horne conducting a band of Choctaws in Arkansas in 1831; the pumpkin field was that of Joseph Kerr in Louisiana, Jahoda, pp. 86-87.

pp. 26-28 Cushman, pp. 165-169, 302-333.

pp. 29-34 Horan, pp. 84-85, Jahoda, pp. 77-78.

pp. 35-40 Jahoda, pp. 267-269, McReynolds, pp. 153-155, 208-209.

pp. 41-45 Jahoda, pp. 273-278.

pp. 46-50 Catlin, pp. 398-403.

pp. 53-59 Jahoda, pp. 301-312; Colin Rickards, *Bowler Hats and Stetsons:*

Stories of Englishmen in the Wild West, New York: Bonanza, pp. 77 ff.

pp. 61-62 Based on my visit to Vršac in Serbia in 1980.

pp. 63-71 Much of the detail from material in the Greenwood LeFlore Public Library, Greenwood, Mississippi and in Ray and Wagner, pp. 141-142. See also the chapter on Greenwood LeFlore in Elizabeth Spencer's *Landscapes of the Heart: A Memoir*, New York: Random House, 1998.

pp.72-81 For the most part the words of Charles Banks Wilson in *A Search for the Purebloods*; the description of some of the dancing, p. 83 from Michael Parfit, "Powwow—a Gathering of the Tribes," *National Geographic*, June 1994, vol. 185, no. 6.

pp. 83-90 W. Richard West quoted in article "Casino Riches Build an Indian Museum with 'Everything'" by Mike Allen in *New York Times*, August 10, 1998, which, together with article "Tribal Windfall: A Chance to Reopen History" by Kay Larson, *New York Times*, July 26, 1998, supplied some of the detail.

Picture Credits

p. ii, p. 2: Ceramic Eagle Warrior (close up of head, p. 4), height 1.68 (66) width 1.19 (47), clay, from Proyecto Templo Mayor, Mexico City, found in the Templo Mayor precinct of Mexico Tenochtitlan in 1982, from H.B. Nicholson with Eloise Quiñones Keber, *Art of Aztec Mexico: Treasures of Tenochtitlan*, Washington: National Gallery of Art, 1983/**p. 10**: Engraving by Albert Dupont, ©1999 by Albert Dupont, from *Le Sentier*, poème visuel de William Jay Smith, traduction française d'Alain Bosquet, Paris: Atelier Albert Dupont, 1999/**p. 15**: George Guess (Sequoyah), Library of Congress, Washington, DC/**p. 20**: Map (Indians of the Southeast: Some routes of removal), from Jesse Burt and Robert B. Ferguson, *Indians of the Southeast: Then and Now*, Nashville, Tennessee: Abingdon Press, 1982/**p. 30**: Pushmataha (The Sapling is Ready for Him), oil on panel, ©The Warner Collection of Gulf State Paper Corporation, Tuscaloosa, Alabama/**p. 36:** Osceola, The Black Drink, A Warrior of Great Distinction, oil on canvas by George Catlin, 1838, ©National Museum of American Art, Washington, DC/Art Resource, NY/**p. 43**: Sorrows of the Seminoles—Banished from Florida, Library of Congress, Washington/**p. 46**: Ball Play of the Choctaws—Ball Up (with Tipis in Background), 1834-1835, oil on canvas by George Catlin, ©National Museum of American Art, Washington, DC/Art Resource, NY/**p. 49**: Drinks of the Juice of the Stone, in Ball-Player's Dress, Choctaw, 1834, oil on canvas, by George Catlin, © National Museum of American Art, Washington DC/Art Resource, NY/ **p. 54**: Buffalo Chase with Bows and Lances, oil on canvas by George Catlin, ©National Museum of American Art, Washington, DC/Art Resource, NY/ **p. 60**: Buffalo Bill on White Horse, c. 1912 (The Farewell Shot) D.F. Barry (1854-1934), hand-colored photograph, ©Buffalo Bill Historical Center, Cody, Wyoming/**p. 61**: Photograph of Sitting Bull, National Museum of American History, National Anthropological Archives (3195-A), Washington, DC /**p. 63**: Photograph of Malmaison, Mississippi Department of Archives and History/**p. 65**: Photograph of Chief Greenwood LeFlore, Mississippi Department of Archives and History/**p. 72**: Kiowa drummer, courtesy Charles Banks Wilson and Gilcrease Museum, Tulsa, Oklahoma/**p. 77**: Seneca man and Cherokee woman, courtesy Charles Banks Wilson and Gilcrease Museum, Tulsa, Oklahoma/ **p. 80**: Kaw man, courtesy Charles Banks Wilson and Gilcrease Museum, Tulsa, Oklahoma/**p. 82**: Buffalo Chase in Winter, Indians on Snowshoes, oil on canvas by George Catlin, ©National Museum of American Art, Washington, DC/Art Resource, NY/**p. 88**: Ms. Coyote by Jean Lamarr, 1992, mixed media mask, courtesy Jean Lamarr and American Indian Contemporary Arts, image courtesy the National Museum of the American Indian, Smithsonian Institution.

WILLIAM JAY SMITH has been a major force in American letters for over half a century. He is the author of more than fifty books of poetry, children's verse, literary criticism, and memoirs, and editor of several influential anthologies. From 1968-1970 he served as Consultant in Poetry to the Library of Congress (a post now called the Poet Laureate) and two of his ten collections of poetry were finalists for the National Book Award.

Smith was born in Louisiana in 1918 and brought up at Jefferson Barracks, just south of St. Louis, Missouri. His memoir, *Army Brat* (1980), which recounts his unusual boyhood as the son of a professional soldier, a clarinctist in the Sixth Infantry Band, was widely acclaimed. He has received the Loines Award for poetry, the California Children's Book and Video Award, the Golden Rose of the New England Poetry Club, and his translations have won awards from the French Academy, the Swedish Academy, and the Hungarian government.

Educated at Washington University, Columbia University, and Oxford (as a Rhodes Scholar), he has been Poet-in-Residence at Williams College, Chairman of the Writing Division of the School of the Arts at Columbia University, and is Professor Emeritus of English at Hollins College. A member of the American Academy of Arts and Letters since 1975 and its former Vice President for Literature, he divides his time between Cummington, Massachusetts, and Paris.

He first became interested in the forced removal of the Southern Indians while exploring his family background and Choctaw heritage for *Army Brat,* and this research was the inspiration for *The Cherokee Lottery.*

CURBSTONE PRESS, INC.

is a non-profit publishing house dedicated to literature that reflects a commitment to social change, with an emphasis on contemporary writing from Latino, Latin American, and Vietnamese cultures. Curbstone presents writers who give voice to the unheard in a language that goes beyond denunciation to celebrate, honor and teach. Curbstone builds bridges between its writers and the public – from inner-city to rural areas, colleges to community centers, children to adults. Curbstone seeks out the highest aesthetic expression of the dedication to human rights and intercultural understanding: poetry, testimonies, novels, stories, and children's books.

This mission requires more than just producing books. It requires ensuring that as many people as possible know about these books and read them. To achieve this, a large portion of Curbstone's schedule is dedicated to arranging tours and programs for its authors, working with public school and university teachers to enrich curricula, reaching out to underserved audiences by donating books and conducting readings and community programs, and promoting discussion in the media. It is only through these combined efforts that literature can truly make a difference.

Curbstone Press, like all non-profit presses, depends on the support of individuals, foundations, and government agencies to bring you, the reader, works of literary merit and social significance which might not find a place in profit-driven publishing channels, and to bring the authors and their books into communities across the country. Our sincere thanks to the many individuals who support this endeavor and to the following businesses, foundations and government agencies: Connecticut Commission on the Arts, Connecticut Arts Endowment Fund, Connecticut Humanities Council, Daphne Seyboldt Culpeper Memorial Foundation, J. M. Kaplan Fund, Eric Mathieu King Fund, Lannan Foundation, Lawson Valentine Foundation, John D. and Catherine T. MacArthur Foundation, National Endowment for the Arts, Open Society Institute, Puffin Foundation, and the Woodrow Wilson National Fellowship Foundation.

Please support Curbstone's efforts to present the diverse voices and views that make our culture richer. Tax-deductible donations can be made by check or credit card to:
Curbstone Press, 321 Jackson Street, Willimantic, CT 06226
phone: (860) 423-5110   fax: (860) 423-9242
www.curbstone.org